INDIAN TRIBES

of the Northwest

by Reg Ashwell

Illustrations by J. M. Thornton

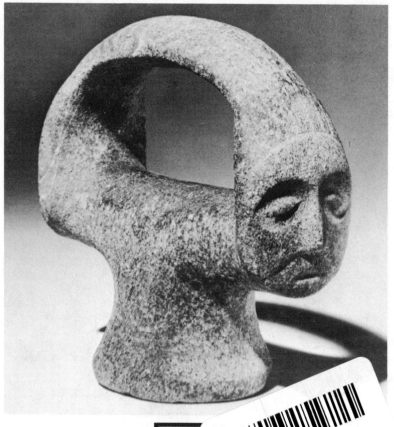

ISBN 0-919654-53-3
Copyright © 1977 Reg Ashwell

Cataloging in Publication Data

Ashwell, Reg, 1921-
    The Indian Tribes of Northwest

Bibliography: p.
Includes index.
    ISBN 0-919654-53-3

    1. Indians of North America — British Columbia. I Title.
E78. B9A85 971.1'004'97 C77-002105-0

FOURTH PRINTING 1983

Published by

HANCOCK HOUSE PUBLISHERS LTD.
19313 Zero Ave., Surrey, B.C. V3S 5J9
HANCOCK HOUSE PUBLISHERS INC.
1431 Harrison Avenue, Blaine WA. 98230

CONTENTS

FOREWORD

Author Reg Ashwell was greatly helped in the preparation of this little booklet by reference to notes he has made over the years after long talks and discourses with such venerable natives as the late Chief August Jack Khatsahlano, and Ellen Neel, among many others. August was the last of forty great Medicine Men, or Witch Doctors, of the ancient Order of Dancers of the Squamish Indians. Ellen was a noble of the Nimpkish band of the Kwakiutl Indians of Alert Bay and the granddaughter of the well known carver, Charlie James. Ellen was destined to become almost as famous as her grandfather and her carved and painted totem poles of yellow cedar are now in museums and private collections all over the world.

Mr. Ashwell was also privileged to enjoy a firm friendship with the late Mildred Valley Thornton, internationally recognized painter of Indian portraiture and author of "Indian Lives and Legends." It was she who, quite apart from imparting much of her own knowledge and wisdom concerning native art and lore, introduced him to many of the Indians who subsequently became his friends.

For the last eight years, Reg Ashwell has been a freelance writer and his articles on British Columbia Indians, and most particularly on Northwest Coast Indian art, have been published in many leading British Columbia newspapers and magazines. He was born at Prince Rupert, British Columbia, on July 12, 1921, and lived with his parents near Terrace in the land of the Tsimshian totem poles, some of which are still standing to this day.

THE INDIAN TRIBES

The origins of the native inhabitants of the Pacific Northwest, from Oregon to Alaska, have never been fully established. It is now believed they migrated from Asia via Siberia over a narrow isthmus of land, which in later times became submerged beneath the waters of the Bering Straits. There may well have been successive waves of migrants who gradually dispersed themselves all over the North and South American continents.

Whatever their beginnings, by the time the first European sailing ships were sighted in our coastal waters, the great northwest was already settled by a diverse people, speaking many different languages and dialects, and with a rich culture of their own. Essentially children of nature, they enjoyed an almost mystical affinity with her forces. Indeed, they saw man and nature as one and this belief profoundly affected their attitude to life. Children were taught never to interfere with, or molest, any living creature. A very old totem pole, which stood for many years at the ancient Haida village of Tanu, graphically illustrates this fact. It was known as the "Weeping Totem Pole of Tanu" and the strange legend surrounding it was told around the lodge fires long before the arrival of the white man.

It all happened on a tragic day long ago, when Chief Always Laughs ruled the people of the northern island of the Queen Charlotte group. Always Laughs was a wise man who knew that the Great Spirit would not deal kindly with people who molested or hurt any creature having life. People could kill for food, but not for pleasure. One day the chief led a hunting party, including seven sons, two grandsons, and seven canoe loads of people to the isle of Tanu to hunt for deer. The hunting party split into small groups and went off to hunt, leaving the two grandsons to guard the fire which had been laboriously lit by rubbing together sticks and tinder against a pile of driftwood gathered for the purpose. When the hunting party returned, they found the fire out. Under questioning, the frightened boys explained that while they were gathering more driftwood they found a large frog and threw it on the fire. It swelled to very large proportions and then burst with a loud bang. After that, the boys gathered all the frogs they could find, both large and small, and threw them on the fire to hear them burst. "But the last frog was the largest," recalled the younger of the boys. "When he burst, he put out the fire!" The chief and his party were horrified. At first they merely lectured the boys, telling them that those who harm the Great Spirit's creatures will surely suffer a similar fate. Finally, overcome by a great

5

foreboding, and urged on by the grieving old chief, the whole party made a dash for their canoes. Not even the fat deer of Tanu could interest them now. But it was too late. As they ran to the shore the earth began to tremble and roar. The ground opened beneath them and the hunting party disappeared. The only person to survive was the old chief, and when he arrived home he became known as "the chief who always weeps for his children." A totem pole, carved from a large cedar tree, was erected in memory of the chief by the remaining relations and tribe. It depicts the chief, wearing his conical ceremonial hat, weeping two very long tears each of which terminates on the head of a grandson. On the chief's breast sits a large frog. The pole was carved with great imagination and power, and became famous among the Haidas, where it was known as the "Weeping Chief Totem of Tanu". Dr. Marius Barbeau, in his comprehensive book "Totem Poles" (Volume 1) which was written for the National Museum, states that it was still standing in the bush when he visited Tanu in 1947. The main portion of the pole, featuring the Weeping Chief, has since been removed to the B.C. Provincial Museum. It remains on view, very old and weathered, yet much admired by visitors.

A splendid replica of the original in its entirety stands outside the main entrance of the B.C. Provincial Museum. It was carved by the Kwakiutl Master Carvers Henry and Tony Hunt in Thunderbird Park in 1966 and was erected in Heritage Court on April 17, 1972. It should be noted, however, that the origins of the Weeping Pole of Tanu (Tanoo) are now lost in time and there are several conflicting legends surrounding the pole.

Francis Poole, the English civil and mining engineer who spent two years among the Haida in the 1860s, complains in his book "Queen Charlotte Islands" of a Haida chief stopping him at his favorite sport of taking pot shots at seals and crows, and ordering him never to do it again. Even today, despite the shattering changes in their life styles during the last century, it is rare indeed to find a native home where you might see a chained dog or a caged bird, and few Indian children show any interest in capturing and molesting wild creatures, although such unnatural behaviour seems to be part of the growing up process with white children.

Instead of great bustling cities of steel and concrete there were only isolated Indian villages scattered along the shorelines and river banks. There were no roads, only a few Indian trails skirting the waterways and rarely penetrating far into the great pathless forests of cedar, fir, spruce, hemlock and pine. Transportation was by canoe or on foot, since in those days the Indians had no horses. In some areas there were vast marshlands, inhabited by many varieties of waterfowl.

Today most of these have been drained off to make room for farm land, housing developments, highways, etcetera, and no longer exist. An

Skidegate 67
P.M'Guire

Weeping Chief Totem of Tanu

example of this is the great Sumas Lake basin. Before the days of the white settlers, great portions of the municipality of Surrey were under a shimmering expanse of shallow water, stretching from just south of New Westminster into the State of Washington. Even supposing the native people had been knowledgeable enough to drain marshes, lakes and ponds, they would probably never have attempted such undertakings. The entire Indian population of British Columbia never stood higher than 100,000 people at any time. But there were other and more subtle reasons which bring us back to the sense of oneness the native people felt environmentally with nature. According to early Indian belief, all living creatures shared in a world of mutual harmony and understanding. The main difference between them was in their external appearance. Strip a bird of his feathers, or the fur from a bear, or the scales from a fish and the form was indistinguishable from human form. To interfere in any way with the environmental dwellings of the salmon people, or the bear people, would be unthinkable and would surely bring swift retribution from the spirits of the creatures involved.

This 'oneness of life philosophy' also led to the concept of 'animal-people' — beings with the characteristics of both.

Picture then, a great beautiful, yet lonely and silent land as it must have been in the days when the great forests were still intact, when the waters literally teemed with fish, and when the skies were sometimes black with myriads of migrating birds. The coastal regions, from Alaska down through British Columbia and into the States of Washington and Oregon, were occupied by a vigorous and extremely creative people to whom we refer as the Indians of the Northwest Coast.

The Coastal Indians of British Columbia were divided into seven linguistic groups, speaking totally different languages and dialects, and yet enjoying a similar culture and life style.

Further inland, where the mild winter rains gave way to snow and bitter cold, life for the Plateau people, the Interior Salish, the Kootenay to the south east and the Athapaskan tribes in the north, was necessarily of a harsher nature and the interior tribes were forced into a nomadic or semi-nomadic existence. These nomadic traits resulted in a less complex social organization due to the fact they were never able to stay in one place long enough to develop it. They were nonetheless a virile and energetic people and were, collectively speaking, as creatively and artistically inclined as their more fortunate cousins on the northwest coast.

TLINGIT

The most northern tribe was the Tlingit, who occupied all of the coastline of southeastern Alaska, from Mount St. Elias to the Portland canal, with the exception of the Prince of Wales Island which had been colonized by the Kaigani Haida shortly before the arrival of the Eurasian voyagers. In such rugged, mountainous and fiorded regions, communication was almost entirely by sea. The Tlingit made fine, well-balanced dugout canoes from red cedar, and made long voyages to trade their sea-otter skins, copper from the Copper River, and hand woven blankets, in exchange for the shell ornaments and slaves which came up to them from the South. Their villages were built close to the water, facing the shoreline. They constructed large gabled plank houses, elaborately carved and decorated with painted designs. The interiors were spacious and comfortable, with the furniture consisting of a number of cedar chests and boxes, some of them exquisitely carved and painted. These were used for storing food and clothing, and masks and rattles and other paraphernalia used in ceremonial dances. There were raised platforms for sitting and sleeping, and these were strewn with skins and cedar bark mats. Placed on shelves beneath the rafters, or stored away in convenient recesses was a miscellaneous assortment of cooking utensils, baskets, horn spoons and ladles, carved wooden bowls and other articles used in their daily lives. Like all the native tribes of coastal British Columbia, the Tlingit were wealthy. Wealth to them, of course, was the wealth provided by nature. The great forests of red cedar gave them their houses, canoes, totem poles, and storage boxes, to name but a few of the uses they had for these tall, straight and mighty trees. The sea literally teemed with salmon (their staple diet), and with halibut, porpoises, seals and sea-otters. Close to the shorelines were the great clam beds and an abundance of seaweed. To supplement their diet still further were numberless roots and berries.

During the summer months the Tlingit devoted most of their time to

Scene in a Tlingit long house showing a Medicine Man performing a shamanistic ritual.   (From an early engraving by W. B. Styles)

hunting and fishing, and taking long journeys in their canoes to trade, and occasionally war, with other tribes. In the winter the men were kept busy doing carpentry work of all kinds, and the women made baskets or wove blankets. The Tlingit people, along with other Northwest Coast tribes, are renowned the world over for their achievements in the plastic arts, and in basketry. Today, the old Tlingit baskets, made from very fine, closely-woven twined spruce root and decorated with strands of maidenhair fern and grasses dyed in natural color, have become very valuable and much coveted by collectors in many parts of the world. But it was the beautiful Chilkat blankets, made from the inner bark of the cedar and from mountain goat wool, and woven by the women from a design drawn by a male artist on a pattern board, which carried the art of the Tlingit to its highest development. Three colors were used; black was obtained from hemlock bark and yellow from tree moss, and a greenish blue was obtained by allowing copper to corrode in urine and then boiling the wool in the resulting liquid. The highly stylized designs on

these blankets, with their intricate patterns and human and animal faces, are very pleasing to the eye. The Tsimshian are usually credited with the early development of the Chilkat blanket, but it was the Tlingit who in historic times made them in large numbers. The collection and preparation of materials, and the subsequent weaving of these fabulous blankets took about a year per blanket. Today they can be seen only in museums and private collections and are now rarely made, the art having almost died with the culture that fostered it.

This interesting photograph of a group of Tlingit Indians posing in ceremonial costumes was taken at Wrangell, Alaska, by G. T. Emmons in 1885. The conventional attire of trousers and leather boots, plainly visible below many of the wearers' blankets, indicates the Tlingit people were already into the process of abandoning their colorful costumes in favor of the white man's style of dress. British Columbia Provincial Museum, Victoria.

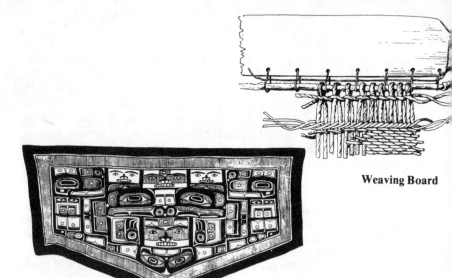

Weaving Board

CHILKAT BLANKET

Although the Tsimshian are credited with being the originators of the Chilkat blanket, it was the Tlingit who in historic times made them in large numbers and carried the art to its highest peak of development.

They were traded down the coast and worn with great pride on ceremonial occasions by the Haida, Tsimshian, Kwakiutl and Bella Coola chiefs and nobles who could afford them.

On the death of the owner they were sometimes placed on the grave and allowed to disintegrate as a mark of esteem.

Chilkat blankets were made from the inner bark of the cedar and from mountain goat wool and were woven by the women from a design drawn by a male artist on a pattern board. It has been recorded that many a heated discussion took place between the artists and the weavers who were trying to interpret the highly stylized totemic designs as closely as possible.

The collection and preparations of materials, and the subsequent weaving of these fabulous blankets, with their bright colors of black, yellow and a greenish blue made from natural dyes, took about a year per blanket.

Tlingit Totem Poles. Museum of Man Nat. Mus.

HAIDA

Slate or argillite totem.

The **Haida** (a name which means simply "people"), were the most powerful tribe of Indians living on the Pacific coast of North America. Living in splendid isolation on the stormy Queen Charlotte Islands and on the southern half of Prince of Wales Island to the north, the Haida frequently raided other tribes in their great war canoes, sometimes paddling as far south as Puget Sound in quest of plunder and slaves.

They were greatly influenced by their nearest neighbors, the Tlingit and Tsimshian tribes, successfully sharing the basketry and shamanistic rituals and songs of the Tlingit. But despite such extensive borrowing from other tribes, they were nonetheless an extremely creative and energetic people. Indeed, it has been said in ethnological circles by some enthusiasts, that the Haida carried Northwest Coast art to its greatest refinement and this superiority was also evident in the construction of their long houses and in the building of their canoes. Like their northern neighbors, they built gable type houses with a partial ridge pole to support the roof, and the planks forming the walls were vertical. The measurements of Haida houses ranged from forty to fifty-five feet in length, and from thirty-five to fifty feet in width; the walls varied from twelve to nineteen feet in height. The carved houseposts in the front walls of the houses stood anywhere from eighteen to fifty-five feet above the ground level, and in the case of a great chief, a second heraldic pole was raised at the back, under the roof beam. In rare cases an oval opening, about three feet high, cut through the lowest section of these heraldic poles, served as an entrance, and provision was also made for an exit at the back of the house.

The canoes varied from small boats manned by one person to great ocean-going canoes, seventy feet long and capable of carrying up to sixty people. As with other Northern tribes in the coastal area, both the bow and the stern of Haida canoes were raised and projected above the water, whereas with the more Southerly tribes in British Columbia, the canoe had a projecting bow but a vertical stern. An awesome and thrilling sight

Haida totem poles at historic old Skidegate. Museum of Man Nat. Mus.

Haida Indian woman weaving a rain hat at the ancient Haida village of Yan on the Queen Charlotte Islands.
These rain-proof hats were made from finely woven spruce root and finished with beautifully painted bird or animal designs in red, blue and black. B.C. Archives.

Haida village at old Skedans 1878 Dawson. Museum of Man Nat. Mus.

Skedans is one of the few abandoned Haida settlements where a few totem poles continue to stand. Battered by wind and weather and swaying uncertainly from their bases, threatened by logging operations, they continue to radiate a stark beauty and power still unextinguished by time.

Haida Shark Mask in Alder by Master Carver Robert Davidson.
The brilliant design of this mask and the artist's careful attention to fine detail including the harmony he has achieved with the wood grain places this work firmly among the highest pinnacles of contemporary Haida art. B.C. Prov. Mus.

Carved from red cedar and highlighted with red and black paint, this pole represents the legend of the berry-picker who was captured by the grizzly bears. Carved almost single-handedly by Robert Davidson, this totem pole has historic significance. The forty-foot totem was raised at the Haida village of old Masset on August 22nd, 1969, and received national press coverage. It was the first totem pole raised on the Charlottes since 1884. David Hancock.
Silver bracelet—also by Robert Davidson.

20

to early voyagers were the ancient Haida villages of Skedans, Tanu, Masset, Skidegate, Yan and others too numerous to mention. The houses were built in a line, close to the shoreline facing the sea, with the great carved totem poles rising high up above the roof tops and the giant canoes, with classic Haida designs frequently painted on the bows and sides, drawn up on the beaches. Monuments indeed to the creative genius of a highly intelligent people.

The Haida did little hunting by land, although occasionally they killed a few of the black bears which ventured into open areas along the coast to eat berries, or feed on salmon at the edges of the streams. But due to their very isolation on the islands they soon became great voyagers and mighty hunters of the sea. They traded heavily with the Tlingit and Tsimshian people, bartering seal furs and sea otter skins and even their magnificent canoes for the coveted Chilkat blankets, and for eulachon oil.

There are no reliable estimates of the Haida population prior to the coming of the white man. Spanish navigators introduced small pox to the Tlingit people as far back as 1775, and epidemics raged up and down the coast taking a heavy toll of their helpless victims. A fairly reliable estimate, taken in 1835, placed the Haida population at around six thousand. Further epidemics, introduced by white settlers in Victoria, took a terrible toll of lives and the Haida were reduced to just a few hundred people by the latter part of the nineteenth century. Missionaries arriving on the Queen Charlottes in the 1800s found a shocked and broken people huddled in two villages, Masset and Skidegate — a far cry from the score or more well-populated areas of earlier days. Missionary influences, backed up by the Colonial government of the day, almost destroyed the old Haida culture and in a few short years only one totem pole was left standing in Skidegate and none at all in Masset. Today, saddened and enlightened British Columbians shake their heads in disbelief that such works of art, including masks, rattles, and other shamanistic paraphernalia, could have been so wantonly destroyed.

But all is not over for the Haida. According to a population census taken in 1973 their numbers had increased to 1500 and are now growing rapidly. Thanks to the determined efforts of a handful of Haida artists like the now legendary Charles Edensaw, and latterly, master carvers and silversmiths Bill Reid and Robert Davidson, the art has not been allowed to die.

The Haida were the only Indians to carve in slate, a carbonaceous shale found only on Slatechuck mountain in the Charlottes, and known to us as argillite. They jealously guard this deposit, and since they control the supply, continue to be the only carvers of argillite, finding a ready market for the glossy black miniature totem poles, ash trays, bowls, and dishes, which in times past were used to barter with the early traders, but which today are bought by collectors and art lovers in the coastal cities of Prince Rupert, Victoria, Vancouver and Seattle.

Symbol of 'Ksan Village

TSIMSHIAN

Another coastal tribe whose territory nevertheless extended much further inland than that of the Tlingit, were the **Tsimshian** ("people inside of the Skeena River"). They were divided into three groups, closely allied one with the other. There were the Tsimshian proper, who lived around the mouth of the Skeena River where it meets the sea, the Gitskan ("Skeena River people"), who lived further up the Skeena, and the Nishga, who inhabited the basin of the Nass River. The art of the Tsimshian people was as prolific and fine as any on the northwest coast. From the mountain goats and sheep they obtained wool for the weaving of blankets and horns for the manufacture of spoons and ladles. The smaller, more delicate spoons were manufactured from the black horns of the mountain goat. By a process of steaming the horn and then fastening it into a mould, bowls were made; the carved handle was often exquisitely carved into animals or birds representing the family crests. Large spoons and ladles were made from the horns of the mountain sheep. Sometimes sheep horn was used for the ladle and goat horn for the handle, making a delightfully pleasing contrast in color and texture. The manufacturing of these wonderful old spoons and ladles was not, of course, confined only to the Tsimshian people. Other northwest coast tribes, notably the Haida and Tlingit, successfully manufactured them. Today they are seldom made and have become extremely valuable and rare, most of them having long since found their way into museums and private collections. Other rare collectors items are the beautiful portrait masks and wooden chests sculptured by the Tsimshian.

The Tsimshian proper, living as they did close to the sea, hunted the seals, sea-lions, and sea-otters, around the islands off the coast, while the Nishga and Gitskan people directed their energies to hunting land animals, such as mountain goats, deer and bears. It has been recorded that in those far-off days the salmon were so thick you could almost walk across the rivers on their backs. Certainly all three groups depended

Drying oolichan. B.C. Archives.

Indian fish traps on the Bulkley river, northern British Columbia. Museum of Man, Nat. Mus.

heavily on the salmon migrations up the rivers every year, salmon being their staple diet, as with most coastal tribes. They also gathered together along the Nass River to fish for oolichan, sometimes known as "candle fish." These small fish, nine to twelve inches long, would arrive at the mouth of the Nass River in incredible numbers. On their arrival they were pursued by seals, sea-lions, and whales, while great flocks of seagulls appeared every day to feed on them until dark. The Tsimshian trapped them in long, bag shaped, wide-mouthed nets. The fish were then boiled by placing hot rocks in large wooden vessels, or even canoes. The water was thus kept boiling until the oil from the fish rose to the surface, where it was recovered after it had cooled. Eulachon oil was highly prized by the natives as a tasty fish sauce, and was also used as a condiment for smoked meats and even such dishes as dried berries. Trade in eulachon was very extensive and long trails, known as "grease trails" led into the interior, where the Tsimshian met and traded with the Athapaskan-speaking tribes. They also traded heavily the coveted oil among other Northwest Coast tribes, transporting it in their canoes.

Tsimshian Rattle. Mus. of Man, Nat. Mus.

'Ksan Village.

**Tsimshian Chief's Chest.
Collected in 1912 on the
Nass river.
B.C. Prov. Mus.**

In their daily lives the Tsimshian people paralleled the Haida in many ways. They had similar customs and beliefs and held feasts and gave great potlatches to celebrate important events, such as the erection of a new totem pole or the assumption of an ancestral name. Medicine-men practised their art and rituals in the same way, acquiring their status either by purification and fasting, as among the Haida, or by sudden and complete recovery from a near fatal sickness. The recovery, of course, being then regarded as positive proof they had the power to heal similar maladies in others.

In 1835 the population of the Tsimshian was estimated at 8,500. By 1895, their lowest year, it had dropped to 3,550 due to the ravages of the white man's diseases. Nevertheless, they were not so hard hit as some of the other northwest coast tribes, probably due to the inland isolation of many of their villages. Many of them greeted the white man's intrusion with cold hostility, and tried to isolate themselves by withdrawing into their villages and attempting as far as possible to hang on to their old ways.

The best stands of totem poles in all of British Columbia are still to be seen in the area of old Hazelton and at Tsimshian villages with such romantic names as Kitwanga, Kitwancool, and Kispiox.

By 1954 the population of the Tsimshian had climbed to 4,802 and is still rapidly growing. With the opening of the model Tsimshian village at 'K san, the arts of the Gitskan and Nishga, and the Coast Tsimshian made a stunning comeback, and the discerning collector can again purchase masks, rattles, storage boxes, small totem poles, and even hand engraved jewelery, comparing very favorably in quality with the work turned out during the latter part of the nineteenth century, when Tsimshian art had developed to its peak.

Tsimshian Indian from the Skeena river area wearing a Chilkat blanket featuring a Killer Whale design and a carved headdress inlaid with abalone shell. In his hands he holds two finely carved rattles with Raven designs. Museum of Man, Nat. Mus.

KWAKIUTL

The **Kwakiutl** Indians occupied the northern corner of Vancouver Island from Johnstone Strait to Cape Cook, and the coast of the mainland from the head of Douglas Channel to Bute Inlet, with the exception of a small area controlled by the Bella Coola people. Of all the Northwest Coast tribes, the Kwakiutl were imaginative people, and these characteristics were graphically mirrored in Kwakiutl art, which, like that of the Bella Coola, was noticeably different from the more stylized work of the Tlingit, Haida, Coast Salish and Tsimshian people. The Kwakiutl did not feel bound by the strict conventions of the Northern art styles, and carved figures on totem poles were not necessarily contained "within the block". Instead they felt free to add beaks, wings, arms, or other appendages, their art being freely rooted in the sculptural traditions of older times on the coast. They loved bright colors and in later times adopted the white man's commercial paints for use when painting designs on their housefronts, masks, and totem poles.

The entire structure of their highly organized society was based on the potlatch, as indeed it was with all of the Northwest Coast tribes. The potlatch was a rather complicated "giving away" ceremony, in which the recipients of lavish gifts were bound to reciprocate by inviting the donors to a return potlatch, where they were bound to prove their standing and influence by giving back far more than they had received. These endless potlatches, and the fantastic ceremonial rituals that were so much a part of it all, fed and encouraged the natural creative urges of the native people.

When the potlatch, along with its accompanying dances and shamanistic rituals, was banned by the government because of its impoverishing effects, the final blow had been delivered and the culture collapsed almost at once.

Kwakiutl Indian woman wearing a woven cloak of shredded cedar bark trimmed with fur. Her face is adorned with two large earrings cut from abalone shell. (E. S. Curtis)

29

A winter view of the Kwakiutl village of Gwayasdums. Photo taken in 1900. Musum of Man, Nat. Mus.

A group of masked dancers taking part in Kwakiutl winter dancing ceremonies 1914. (E. S. Curtis)

Potlatch Copper incised and engraved with human face and hands. Nat. Mus.

large pile of blankets arranged for a tlatch at Alert Bay around the turn of century.

A scene from one of the last great Potlatches held at Alert Bay, on tiny Cormorant Island, B.C. B.C. Prov. Mus.

31

Quatsino woman and canoe. E. S. Curtis.

Inspecting newly carved Kwakiutl Dance
Masks at Thunderbird Park.
Seen at left is the renowned Kwakiutl Master
Carver the late Mungo Martin. B.C. Gov't.

A Quatsino woman with flattened forehead. This deformation was considered a mark of beauty. A pad, usually of cedar bark, was attached to the baby's cradle and bound against the forehead. By slow pressure over a period of time, the forehead was gradually flattened. Mus. of Man, Nat. Mus.

But the Kwakiutl, perhaps a little more assertive in their character than other tribes, did not give up easily. They went underground, carrying on the secret society dances and even the potlatches, as best they could in undeveloped areas where they were not likely to be caught. Some were eventually jailed for it, yet the old customs never really died among the Kwakiutl. Unlike other tribes, they never did stop carving totem poles, and a very fine stand of them, showing Kwakiutl art at its greatest development, can be seen at Alert Bay where a truly splendid memorial pole, carved by master carvers Henry and Tony Hunt, was raised in 1970 to honor master carver Mungo Martin. Significantly, the project received the whole-hearted support of the government, a far cry from the policy of colonial days.

BELLA COOLA

Frontlet mask. Mus. of Man Nat. Mus.

Hemmed in on three sides by the Kwakiutl, and indeed, jutting into Kwakiutl territory to a point where it almost divided them in two, was the land of the **Bella Coola** people. Their villages faced the Dean and Bella Coola Rivers, and were also built along the fiords into which these rivers flow. Each village contained anywhere from two to thirty plank houses built in a row facing the waterfront, and each house sheltered from two to ten families. The Bella Coola were originally a Salish-speaking people who possibly broke away from the main body to the south of them, and trekked across the mountains to their present location. Their staple diet was salmon and oolichan, but they also ate wild goats, geese, ducks, bears, porcupines, and seals, as well as enjoying an abundance of wild berries and roots.

The Bella Coola were understandably greatly influenced by both the interior Apathepascan to the east and their Kwakiutl neighbors. Bella Coola art has often been linked with that of the Kwakiutl, but there were subtle differences, usually fairly obvious to the trained eyes of ethnologists and collectors of native art. The differences were especially obvious in their beautiful totems, splendid examples of which can be seen at the provincial museum in Victoria. Like the Kwakiutl, the Bella Coola carved masks depicted great mythical monster birds. These masks, which were sometimes up to five feet in length, had very long movable beaks which would clack in lively fashion when concealed ropes were pulled. They were brightly decorated with red, white, black, and green or blue paint, and heavily fringed with long strands of shredded cedar bark and were used extensively in the secret society dances.

The Bella Coola were never numerous and the population census of 1835 listed only 2,000 of them. By 1929 they had been reduced by the white man's diseases to a shocking total of only 249 people, but since then have gradually increased in numbers and the population in 1954 stood at 385 and still continues to rise.

Bella Coola Village. Circa 1895. B C. Prov. Mus.

Interior of long house showing raised platform. Village of Komskotes, Mus. of Man Nat. Mus.

Petroglyph, Bella Coola River. Mus. of Man Nat. Mus.

Memorial Pole

The Prairie Indian, with his colorful headdress of eagle feathers, his leggings and moccasins and tunic of deer skin, remains the stereotype of the white man's image of the noble aboriginal of long ago. But the facts are that the Coastal tribes wore neither feathered headdresses, leggings nor moccasins, and in fine weather the men preferred to go around totally naked. Yet never were a people so imbued with love of decoration and design. Indeed, when clothing was worn it was usually for decorative effect, or as a slight protection against rain. The usual form of headgear was in the shape of a truncated cone with a wide, flared base. These hats, made from spruce roots or cedar fibres, were often exquisitely woven works of art, beautifully painted with bird or animal designs, cleverly adapted to the shape of the hat. For ceremonial occasions, chiefs and nobles of the tribe who could afford them, wore carved and painted wooden helmets or headdresses, sometimes intricately inlaid with abalone shell and with white fur pelts fastened to the sides and back, giving a grand effect as they hung in snowy splendor around the shoulders of the wearer.

Chief Maquinna.

NOOTKA

When we refer to the arts of the Indians of the Northwest Coast, we usually mean the five northern tribes comprising the Tlingit, Haida, Tsimshian, Kwakiutl and Bella Coola. Little has been documented on Nootkan art; yet the Nootka people, inhabiting the west coast of Vancouver Island from Cape Cook to Port San Juan, were also a vigorously creative and artistic tribe.

In past times they were divided into twenty-five different groups. Twenty-four of these groups dwelt in British Columbia and the remaining group, the Makah, lived on the northern Washington coast.

The Nootka were courageous whalers and it is highly probable that they were the only tribe to regularly hunt the great whales. Nootka men were trained from early childhood in the management of their sturdy dugout canoes, and frequently paddled beyond sight of the stormy coastline in search of their ocean prey. Fish, particularly salmon, herring and halibut, furnished the main food supply, but they also hunted seals, sea-lions, and sea-otters while women and children dug for clams along the sea shore, or gathered roots and berries for further variety in the diet.

Clothing, when worn at all, was similar to other coastal tribes. The women wore a fringed skirt, woven from shredded cedar bark. Nootka men usually preferred to go around without clothing of any kind, although sometimes in rainy weather they wore a cape of cattails or cedar bark. For special occasions, the nobles of the tribe wore robes of bearskin, lynx, or marten; even more beautiful were robes made by the women from the inner bark of the cedar, and edged with otter fur. The hats worn by Nootka men were also made by the women from very finely woven spruce root or cedar bark fibers. Clever designs were woven into the hats, rather than painted on them, as with the more Northern tribes. These designs often depicted a whale hunt, with warriors in canoes attempting to harpoon the whale, sometimes under the watchful eyes of the mighty Thunderbird (a mythical spirit-bird in the form of an eagle,

Nootka Whaler (E. S. Curtis)

Nootka dancers wearing masks representing legendary mythical Nootka monster birds 1914. (E. S. Curtis)

A scene inside a Nootka long house, Nootka Sound, British Columbia. B.C. Archives.

Nootka Totem Pole, Friendly Cove

Section of a Nootka Totem Pole at an abandoned Nootka village on Esperanza inlet, Graveyard Bay. The power and stark beauty of Nootka art is revealed in this close-up view of a bear holding a frightened man between his paws.

Indian Burial Cave

Two Nootka women gaze at the carcass of a whale off Washington coast (E. S. Curtis)

Clayoquot woman making basket by C. F. Newcome in 1903. B.C. Prov. Mus.

famous in Nootka legends and among other Northwest Coast tribes, notably the Kwakiutl and Salish).

The Nootka built huge plank houses, usually with flat, shed-type roofs, and like their Kwakiutl neighbors, had carved inside house-posts supporting the roof beams. They did not begin carving outside totem poles until the latter part of the nineteenth century, and this practice soon ceased under the influence of early missionaries. However, there are a few poles still standing in the vicinity of ancient Nootkan villages and graveyards, which although weathered with age, and minus most of the paint which once so complimented and adorned them, continue to reveal a stark beauty and to emanate a power reminiscent of the work of more Northerly coastal tribes.

Nootka women are justly famous for the high quality of their basketry, with splendid designs depicting whale hunts and Nootka legends of the Wolf and Thunderbird or perhaps the mythical Hai-et-lik, the Lightning Snake. These baskets, woven of bear or sweet grass, are still made but with not so fine a weave as in the past.

The rather vague population census taken in 1835 estimated the Nootka people as numbering around 7,500. Their lowest year was in 1939, when the population declined to only 1,605. But by the time the next census was taken in 1954, their numbers had increased to 2,100, a healthy increase which still continues.

COAST SALISH

Outside House Post. Mus. of Man.

The **Coast Salish** Indians were neighbors of the Nootka and Kwakiutl people, but did not exercise the same interest shown by them in carving and painting. They inhabited the coast of the mainland, from Bute Inlet to the Columbia River, and those areas on Vancouver Island not occupied by the Kwakiutl and the Nootka from Johnstone Strait to Port San Juan. Historically the Coast Salish Indians did not carve totem poles, although carved "welcoming figures," house-posts, and mortuary figures were noted by early pioneers. These welcoming figures, standing ten to twenty feet in height, were an awesome sight and caused much comment among travelers seeing them for the first time. The figure was that of a man, sometimes wearing a hat and short cape, but usually nude with pegged on arms, both of which were raised in a welcoming salute. Some splendid examples of these, and other Salish carvings, can be seen at the Provincial Museum in Victoria.

Coast Salish women made fine baskets, with imbricated designs. They also wove handsome, fringed blankets from the sheared wool of a small, white dog which was kept for that purpose and is now extinct.

These strange little white woolly dogs were kept by the Coast Salish, who placed a high value on the hair which was similar to sheep's wool. The dogs were shorn of their coats at intervals, and the wool used (usually along with that of the mountain goat) in the weaving of Salish blankets. With the arrival of the white traders and the subsequent establishment of Hudson's Bay trading posts, the Salish people were soon able to acquire the famous Hudson's Bay blankets and no longer found it necessary to go through the tedious process of weaving their own on primitive looms.

The dogs were no longer a valuable commodity, and soon became extinct, probably due to interbreeding with dogs brought in by white settlers and gradually acquired by the Indians as pets.

A Masked Cowichan Dancer. He is wearing a Skhway Khwey Mask. These famous masks are still used in Coast Salish ceremonial dances. E. S. Curtis.

45

Cowichan loom and woven blanket of goat hair. B.C. Archives.

Spindle Whorl. Mus. of Man Nat. M▶

Knitting the famous Cowichan Indian Sweaters. B.C. Gov't.

Coast Salish Canoes on the Songhees Reserve looking south at Esquimalt, Victoria. B.C. Archives.

The Salish produced beautiful natural dyes for coloring their blankets with attractive geometrical patterns. Alder bark was used for red; lichen for yellow cedar and hemlock bark for brown; Oregon grape for a yellow-green and copper for blue-green.

For dress-up occasions and ceremonies, Salish men sometimes wore a high conical hat, made of human hair and crowned with two duck or loon feathers which were cleverly fastened to a short spindle embedded in the pinnacle of the hat. The slightest movement of the wearer would cause the feathers to sway rhythmically back and forth. These hair hats were used in spirit dance ceremonies along with a beautiful buckskin costume sewn with tiny paddles.

The staple diet of the Coast Salish, as with other coastal tribes, was fish supplemented by the meat of wild goats and deer.

They built shed type houses with flat roofs, which inclined upwards from front to rear, or vice versa. The great width of these shed houses, forty feet or more, gave the roofs a gentle pitch. This made the roofs very useful for drying fish and also provided a handy platform for spectators at potlatches, and other ceremonial gatherings and festivities!

The Coast Salish were the most numerous of all the coastal tribes. In British Columbia alone the population census of 1835 placed their numbers at 12,000. By 1915, their low year, the usual plagues and diseases had reduced the population to 4,120. However, there has been a healthy increase in numbers among the Coast Salish in recent years and in 1954 the population stood at 6,397 and has continued to rise steadily.

Nat. Mus.

INTERIOR SALISH

The **Interior Salish** Indians were dissimilar in many ways to their Coast Salish neighbors. They had different customs, they spoke in different languages and dialects, and according to some sources, even differed in physical appearance. The Interior Salish were not a united people. They were divided into five tribes which were continuously battling with each other. There were first the Lillooet or Wild Onion Indians of the Lillooet River valley. Second, the Thompson River Indians, inhabiting the Fraser River valley from Yale to Lillooet, and on the Thompson River as far up as Ashcroft. Third, the Okanagan Indians of the Okanagan Lake and River, and fourth, the Lake Indians of the Arrow Lakes and Upper Columbia River. Fifth and last, were the Shuswap Indians, controlling the Fraser River valley from Lillooet to Alexandria, and all the country eastward to the summits of the Rocky Mountains.

Collectively speaking, and despite their small wars with each other, the Interior Salish formed the largest linguistic group in the interior of British Columbia and their territory extended well south into the States of Washington and Idaho. They did a little carving and painting but never approached the levels achieved by the coastal tribes in artistic skills. Yet the women of all five tribes excelled in the craft of basketry. They decorated their baskets externally with beautifully imbricated designs of red and black cherry bark and white bulrush, with wonderful zig-zag patterns representing waves or arrowheads and including animals, birds, and insects. The only other people who made comparable baskets were the Chilcotin and some of the Coast Salish, both of whom learned the art from the Interior Salish.

The winter home of these people was a circular semi-subterranean house, around forty-five feet in diameter, which was entered by a notched log from the roof. The summer home was an oblong or conical lodge covered with rush mats. Both the summer and winter dwellings,

Interior Salish girl with her hair specially braided to mark the termination of her adolescence. Mus. of Man Nat. Mus.

A Thompson River Indian handsome and finel featured, poses in magnificent headdress o eagle feathers and beade and fringed buckski costume complete wit moccasins, in front of hi lodge. Mus. Man

A fairly typical summer home of the Thompson River Indians showing a conical shaped lodge covered with rush mats. Mus. of Man Nat. Mus.

An Interior Salish basket weaver photographed in the Fraser River area in 1902. B.C. Prov. Mus.

with their dark and airless interiors, were in stark contrast to the great, spacious lodges built from red cedar by the coastal tribes. Because of their nomadic nature the larger, more permanent homes were unsuitable. This nomadic trait resulted in a less complex social organization— primarily because they simply were not in one place long enough to develop it.

Due to the harsher climate of the interior, the Interior Salish were forced to wear protective clothing in order to keep warm. During the summer months the women wore a kind of tunic and the men nothing but a breech-cloth. But for cold weather they had robes of fur, leggings, and moccasins of dressed skin. For traveling, some families had dug-outs similar to the river canoes used in the delta of the Fraser by the coast people. But most of them preferred the easily-made bark canoes. Most of their journeys, however, had to be made on foot due to the dangerous rapids of the turbulent Fraser and Columbia Rivers, and their tributaries.

Salmon remained the principal source of food, but cut off as they were from the sea-mammals, the Interior Salish hunted and trapped the land animals extensively. Bear, beaver, marmot, elk and deer were prominent in their diet.

They traded heavily with the Coast Salish, bartering hemp, skins, bark, and goat's wool for shells, slaves, smoked beach foods; and occasionally dug-out canoes.

The population of the Interior Salish dropped drastically from an estimated 13,500 in 1835 to 5,348 in 1890 and even at that they fared better than the Coastal tribes, who were more exposed to the white man's diseases. By 1954 their numbers had climbed again to 7,711 and they continue to increase. Like most other Indian tribes they are developing a growing pride in their cultural identity.

Chiefs of the Thompson River Indians posing in full regalia. Mus. of Man Nat. Mus.

The **Kootenay** Indians, tall and fine-featured, re
tribes, in dress, customs and religion. Indeed, it has bee
they dwelt on the Eastern side of the Rockies until the
eighteenth century but were harassed and driven we
Blackfoot who forced them to retreat across the mountains
again in the Northern part of the State of Idaho, and the
corner of British Columbia between the Rocky Mountai
Selkirks, from about latitude forty-nine degrees North, to
degrees North. They seem to have divided themselves into two
the Upper Kootenay, of the upper Columbia and upper Kootenay
who frequently crossed the mountains to hunt the buffalo o
prairies, and the Lower Kootenay of the lower Kootenay River,
spoke a slightly different dialect, and being further removed from
mountains, seldom joined in the buffalo hunts, and subsisted mainly o
fish.

Like the Plains Indians, they wore beautiful headdresses of eagle
feathers and their dress was entirely of skin, consisting of a shirt, breech-
cloth, leggings, and moccasins.

Their dwellings, like those of the Blackfeet and other Plains Indians,
were the conical tepees or wigwams, with buffalo hides or rush mats
stretched around a framework of long poles.

The Kootenay also emulated the Plains people by painting designs
on their tepees, garments, and even their bodies. Many of those designs
reflected elements seen in power-visions, dreams or guardian-spirit
guests.

The Lower Kootenay were affected to a certain extent by the
customs of the neighboring Salish, from whom they probably learned the
art of making watertight baskets of split roots. Both the Lower and
Upper Kootenay used bark canoes which were substantially different
from the Interior Salish craft, and their cooking utensils were of birch
bark.

**An old photo of Chief Paul Daird of the Kootenay Indians in Utlak dress. Mus.
of Man Nat. Mus.**

Portion of a camp circle of cloth tepees typical of the Kootenay and Plains people. 1915. Museum of Man Nat. Mus.

Old photograph of Kootenay Indian pageantry.

Cleaning salmon.

Indian Travois. The travois was a primitive sled constructed between a framework of two poles that served as a shaft for the horse. It was used extensively by nomadic Indians as an ingenious method of transporting their belongings when changing camp. Mus. of Man Nat. Mus.

They were a happy, peaceful, and contented people, although few in numbers. Only about a thousand of them were counted in the population census taken in 1835, and over the next century their numbers gradually dwindled to an all-time low of 381 (according to the census of 1939). Fifteen years later a slight improvement was recorded, with the population increasing to 424, and it is still climbing, albeit very slowly.

When the Kootenay retreated from the Blackfeet and crossed the mountains into British Columbia and Idaho, they brought their horses, and to this day they remain accomplished horsemen. British Columbia is fortunate in having a small corner where a breath of the color and pageantry associated with the Plains Indians can continue to flourish in the land of the kindly and intelligent Kootenay people.

Athapaskan speaking tribes

Life for the Athapaskan speaking tribes of the central and northern areas of the British Columbia interior was harsh, especially during the long, hard winter months which in some of the Northernmost regions lasted from September until April. They were of necessity a wandering, semi-nomadic people, constantly in search of food and with little time or inclination for the cultural amenities enjoyed by the coastal tribes.

A Carrier Indian Chief at a Fort St. James pageant in 1928. B.C. Archives.

61

CHILCOTIN

The **Chilcotin** are the southernmost of the tribes of Athapaskan origin. They were spread over the country from the Cascade Mountains to near the Fraser River, and were known as a bold, restless, and turbulent people, constantly at enmity with their Carrier kinsmen to the north. Culturally, socially, and economically, they were much better off than their Athapaskan cousins. Surrounded, as they were, by the Salishan tribes on their Southern and Eastern flanks, and by the Kwakiutl and Bella Coola to the West, they derived much of their social and material life from these neighboring peoples, at the same time clinging tenaciously to their own language and customs.

Food supplies were fairly plentiful—bears, wild goats and sheep, caribou, marmots, and rabbits were trapped and hunted, and there were many varieties of edible roots and berries. The Chilcotin also traded heavily with their neighbors, particularly the Bella Coola, for salmon and the other necessities they lacked. It was this trading with other surrounding tribes that led to so many other exchanges, resulting in the Chilcotin culture becoming a blend of elements from different sources.

Their winter homes were rectangular, earth covered lodges, walled and roofed with bark and brush. Some of them preferred to emulate the Shuswap and built small subterranean houses for use as winter dwellings.

Clothing was similar to that of other Athapaskan tribes — belt, breech-cloth (or skirts for women), leggings, and moccasins. During the cold weather they wore caps and robes of fur.

The Chilcotin women learned the art of basketry from the Shuswaps, but the beautifully imbricated designs, which frequently included deer and other wild life, were peculiarly their own.

Two Indian babies stare wide-eyed from their cradles. B.C. Archives.

CARRIER

The **Carrier** Indians were remote kinsmen of the Chilcotin and lived directly north of them. They roamed over the country of the Upper Fraser, Blackwater, Nechako, and Bulkley Rivers, as far north as Bear Lake. The Carrier derived their name from the strange and cruel custom they had of compelling widows to carry the charred bones of their dead husbands on their backs, like bundles of firewood for a minimum period of two years. They were an austere and hardy people, greatly influenced in their social and political life by the Tsimshian even to the point of copying Tsimshian noblemen in the practise of carving their crests on the pillars of their houses, yet lacking the artistic and creative ability of the Coast tribes.

Their staple diet was fish since all the rivers fairly teemed with salmon during the summer months and the lakes abounded with trout which could be caught under the ice during the hard winters. They also hunted bears, beavers, rabbits, marmots and caribou, and like most other native tribes throughout British Columbia, gathered berries and roots whenever they were available.

A Carrier Indian scraping a moose hide. Mus. of Man Nat. Mus.

They traded with the Tsimshian, and other coast tribes, to obtain the coveted Chilcat blankets, copper bracelets, and shell ornaments. Yet they dressed much like the Chilcotin and other Athapaskan tribes, with skin robes, leggings, and moccasins.

Some of the southern Carrier passed the long winter months in underground lodges, similar to those of the Chilcotin and Shuswap. The remainder, however, preferred to build rectangular structures above ground, roofed with spruce bark, and gabled at the front and back by the continuation of the roof down to the ground on each side, thus omitting the upright walls.

Warriors used the same weapons as the surrounding tribes — bows and arrows, lances, clubs, and knives. Hunting parties communicated with each other by making much use of graphic signs inscribed on rocks which could be easily interpreted and understood by the beholder.

SEKANI

North of the Carrier Indians, and frequently harassed by them, lived the **Sekani** (people of the rocks). They controlled the basins of the Parsnip and Finlay Rivers, and the valleys of the Peace as far down as the present-day town of Peace River. Since supplies of fish were none too plentiful, they became great hunters, living by the chase, and with no permanent villages. They lived mostly on moose, bear, porcupine, caribou, beaver, and any smaller game they could catch. They erected rude conical lodges of poles, covered with spruce bark, or sometimes merely lean-tos, overlaid with bark, skins, or brush. The men wore a kind of sleeveless shirt of skin, sometimes laced together between the legs in lieu of a breech-cloth, leggings that reached to the thighs, and moccasins with insoles of ground-hog, or rabbit fur. Women wore a similar costume, except that they either lengthened the shirt, or added a short apron, and their leggings only came as high as the knees. For winter warmth they wore robes, caps, and mittens. Hunters liked to adorn themselves with grizzly bear claws, and both men and women wore bracelets of horn and bone, while shirts and moccasins were often embroidered with porcupine quills.

The nomadic Sekani were harassed in their efforts to expand by the Cree and Beaver Indians on their Eastern flank, and by the Carrier and Shuswap tribes to the South of them. Nevertheless, they traveled Westward, and occupied the territory around Bear Lake and the northern end of Takla Lake, and even managed to establish a village on the Tachick River, in close proximity to the Carrier of Stuart Lake. This expansion took place around the end of the eighteenth century, before the arrival of white traders and trappers which spelled doom for the unfortunate Sekani. White trappers and miners, bringing with them their alcohol and diseases, invaded Sekani territory and hunted their game, which soon became less plentiful. The tribe became demoralized, disease-ridden, and undernourished, and rapidly decreased in numbers almost to the point of extinction.

A bark lodge of the Sekani Indians. Mus. of Man Nat. Mus.

TAHLTAN

Neighbors of the Sekani, yet much closer to the Carrier in their dress and general mode of life, were the **Tahltan** Indians. They occupied the extreme Northern interior of British Columbia, including the country from the Cascade Mountains to the Cassiar River, thus giving them control of the entire drainage basin of the upper Stikine River, and the headwaters of some of the streams that fed the Taku, Nass, Skeena, MacKenzie, and Yukon Rivers. Because of the dry climate and resulting light snowfall in winter, they were able to continue hunting the year round. But large timber was scarce, and the Tahltans were constantly forced to migrate in search of fuel. The shortage of timber created other hardships for them. They were able to make only a few birch bark canoes, and these of such poor quality that the temporary rafts they were forced to construct to ferry themselves across the numerous streams, were almost as useful. Their simple dwellings were usually mere lean-tos of poles, laid closely together, roofed with bark, and packed with earth and boughs around the bottom. Yet each of the six clans in the tribe owned a lodge for a permanent dwelling, one hundred feet or more in length, with vertical walls and a roof of bark. These large houses sheltered all the principal families of the clan, and were useful as halls for potlatches and dances. They were located only in the Tahltan's principal village on the Tahltan river.

Tahltan Sweat House at Casca Flats,, near Telegraph Creek. Mus. of Man Nat. Mus.

Babiche Bag.

Tahltan Indian Moccasins.
Mus. of Man Nat. Mus.

The Stikine River valley, below Telegraph Creek, was shared by the Tahltan with the Tlingit, who caught salmon and gathered berries there during the summer months, whereas the Tahltan hunted over it during the winter after the Tlingit had returned to the coast. Grassland and stony ridges covered much of the Tahltan country, yet it was rich in game and large shoals of salmon annually ascended the Stikine river. The Tahltans would scatter to the hunting grounds in early winter, then gather towards spring at the fishing grounds to await the arrival of the salmon. In the fall they assembled on the Stikine River to trade and barter with the Tlingit, and to enjoy the festivities which followed.

The Tahltan also traded with the Kaska Indians, exchanging moose and caribou hides, sinew thread, leather bags, babiche, and various furs, for other items of trade.

BEAVER

In early times, the customs of the **Beaver** Indians did not differ greatly from those of the Sekani. Until about the middle of the eighteenth century the Beaver occupied not only the entire basin of the Peace River below its junction with the Smoky, but the district around Lake Claire and the valley of the Athabaskan River as far south as the Clearwater and Methy portage. Around 1760, however, they were attacked by bands of Cree (provided with firearms by the furtraders on Hudson Bay), and swept from the valley of the Athabaska and confined to the basin of the Peace. The eastern Beaver then made a truce with the Cree, consequently adopting their dress and many of their customs. They never attempted to regain their lost territories since the fur posts established soon afterwards took care of all their needs.

The western Beaver, moving further up the Peace River, managed to displace the Sekani from the mouth of the Smoky River to Rocky Mountain Canyon, and continued to maintain their old customs for several decades.

Like all of the Athapaskan people of northern Canada, the Beaver had no real unity, but were divided into separate bands that roamed over separate hunting territories. Moose, caribou, beaver, and other game abounded, and there were numerous buffalo, which the Indians drove into pounds, after the manner of the Plains tribes. Yet they appear to have esteemed the buffalo less highly than the moose, which gave them not only meat, but skins for clothing and for the covers of their tents. These tents were the conical, tepee-like structures common throughout the basin of the MacKenzie, which the Sekanis covered with spruce bark, but most of the other tribes covered with caribou skins.

KASKA

Little has been documented about the Nahani Indians who once inhabited the mountainous area between the upper Liard River and the sixty-fourth parallel North latitude (according to Diamond Jenness in his "Indians of Canada"). Many Nahanis were once treacherously massacred by the Slave Indians, who drove the remainder into the mountains. Originally, they were divided into several independent bands, most of which have now disappeared altogether. But from about Mc-Dame Creek on Dease River, to the Beaver River that joins the Liard above Liard, dwelt two bands known as the **Kaska** Indians, the Tsezotene, Mountain People on the West, and the Titshotina, Big Water people on the East. In their way of life, and indeed in most of their customs and religious beliefs, the Kaska differed but little from the Sekani in the South, or from the tribes along the MacKenzie. Nevertheless, the geographical position of the Kaska near the headquarters of the Stikine River, exposed them to influences coming from the Pacific Coast. They learned to weave the hair of the wild mountain goat into ropes, game bags, and even robes, ornamented with beautiful blue and green designs.

The Kaska lived principally by the chase, using bows and arrows, spears and clubs, and most especially snares of twisted sinew or babiche.

Like most of the Northern tribes, the Kaska believed in a guardian spirit, acquired through dreams, to aid them in times of trouble. They copied the Tahltan and Tlingit in cremating their dead, but later abandoned this practise in favor of burial in the ground.

SLAVE

According to Alexander Mackenzie, the **Slave** Indians were neighbors of the Beaver in the eighteenth century, and inhabited Athabaska Lake, Slave River, and the western half of Great Slave Lake. When the Cree Indians invaded this area the Slave were forced to retreat down the Mackenzie River, and by the end of the century occupied a broad stretch of country behind both banks of that river from its outlet at Great Slave Lake to Norman, the basin of the lower Liard, and the West end of Great Slave Lake.

The Slave Indians preferred to cling to the forests, and seldom ventured out onto the barren grounds. They used snares to trap all animals except the beaver, which they captured in wooden traps in the fall. Nearly half the diet of the Slave Indians consisted of fish, which they ingeniously caught in nets of twisted willow bark, or with lines of the same material fitted with hooks of wood, bone, or antler, and even occasionally bird's claws.

Their clothing was similar to that of the Beaver, but much more ornamental, with great use of porcupine quills and moose hair, and more heavily bordered with fringes. Moccasins were joined to the leggings and the men wore some sort of a tassel rather than a breech cloth. Around the mouth of the Liard, where woodland caribou and moose were less plentiful, the majority of the women wore garments of woven hare-skin, a material which they also used for cradle-bags. Both sexes, with their great love of ornamentation, adorned themselves with armlets of leather, embroidered with porcupine quills. Men added necklets of polished caribou antler, and sometimes passed a goose quill or perhaps a plug of wood, through the septum of the nose.

When on the warpath, the men wore headdresses of bear claws, or caps ringed with feathers, and protected their bodies with wooden shields and cuirasses of willow twigs.

The Slave used stone adzes, shafted to wooden handles, for cutting down trees, and knives with beaver-tooth blades for whittling wood and bone. For cooking, women used vessels of spruce roots, heated by means of hot stones.

It is said that surrounding tribes rarely ventured to attack the Slave Indians, fearing the great skill attributed to them in witchcraft. Yet on the whole they had the reputation of being a peaceful, happy and inoffensive people.

When we refer to the Athapaskan-speaking tribes of British Columbia, (the Chilcotin, Carrier, Sekani, Tahltan, Beaver, Kaska, and Slave Indians) we must not lose sight of the fact that they were a scattered and diverse people, in no way united, and apart from similar dialects spoken by the tribes, felt little kinship with each other, and indeed, fought many skirmishes along their tribal borders. Collectively, they numbered about 8,800 when the population census was taken in 1835. Sixty years later their numbers had dwindled to 3,716 due to disease, alcohol, and in the case of the Sekani at least, starvation. But by 1954 the population had climbed again and stood at 5,152, and there has been a continuing improvement through the years.

hancock

house

74

FURTHER REFERENCES

A CORNER STONE OF CANADIAN CULTURE by Alice Ravenhill, from Occasional Papers of the British Columbia Provincial Museum.

ARTIFACTS OF THE NORTHWEST COAST INDIANS by Hilary Stewart

ARTS OF THE RAVEN CATALOG, The Vancouver Art Gallery, Catalog text by Wilson Duff, with contributory articles by Bill Holm and Bill Reid.

IMAGES: STONE: B.C. by Wilson Duff and Hilary Stewart.

INDIAN ART AND CULTURE by Della Kew and P. E. Goddard.

INDIANS OF CANADA by Diamond Jenness, Bulletin 65, Anthropological Series No. 15, National Museum of Canada.

INDIANS OF THE NORTHWEST by D. Allen.

INDIANS OF THE PACIFIC NORTHWEST by Ruth Underhill.

INDIAN PETROGLYPHS OF THE PACIFIC NORTHWEST by Beth and Ray Hill.

NATIVE TRIBES OF BRITISH COLUMBIA by Alice Ravenhill.

PEOPLE OF THE POTLATCH by Audrey Hawthorne, Museum of Anthropology, University of British Columbia.

THOSE BORN AT KOONA by John and Carolyn Smyly.

TOTEM POLES BULLETIN 119 Volumes 1 and 2 by Dr. Marius Barbeau, published by the National Museum of Canada.

TOTEM POLES OF THE NORTHWEST by D. Allen.

PRINTED IN CANADA